WHAT'S BENEATH
PEEKING UNDER
the CITY

by Esther Porter

illustrated by Andrés Lozano

raintree

a Capstone company — publishers for children

Welcome to the big city!
Do you see the tall buildings and bright lights?
See the people hurrying up and down the streets?
Hear the music, sirens and car horns?

So much happens in a city ABOVE ground. What happens BELOW?
Turn the page to peek beneath ...

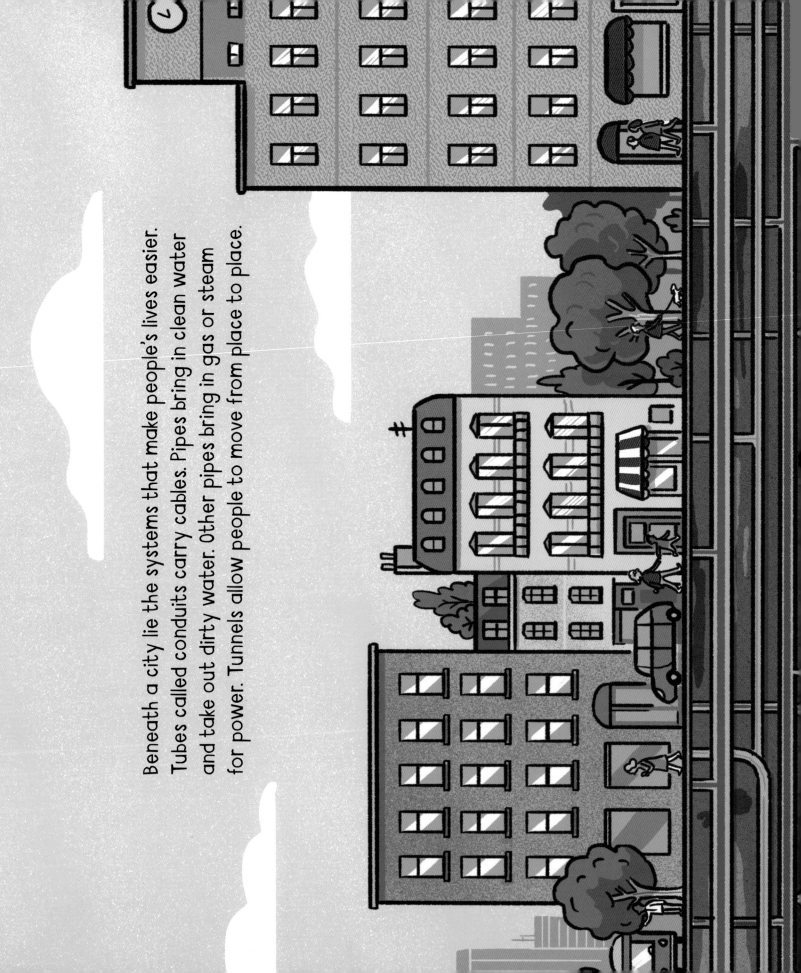

Beneath a city lie the systems that make people's lives easier. Tubes called conduits carry cables. Pipes bring in clean water and take out dirty water. Other pipes bring in gas or steam for power. Tunnels allow people to move from place to place.

All of these systems are carefully planned. Civil engineers do the planning. They work closely with builders to decide where everything needs to go.

Power up!

What are all these lines? Thousands of kilometres of cables! Most cables run underground. Burying cables keeps them safe from wind, rain and ice. Some cables carry power to homes and businesses. Others carry information for computers and TVs.

wind turbines

solar farm

river dam

power station

DID YOU KNOW?

Power comes from many places. Coal-burning power stations make electricity. So do solar farms, wind turbines and river dams. Electricity flows into a city through cables.

Thirsty?

People need clean water for drinking, washing and cooking. Where does it come from?

Water comes from lakes, rivers and reservoirs. It's cleaned in water treatment plants. Then it's piped into a city. Water flows first through large pipes called mains. Smaller pipes called sub-mains carry water from the mains to branch lines. Branch lines carry water into buildings. In large cities more than 3.8 billion litres (1 billion gallons) of water may flow every day.

DID YOU KNOW?

New York City, USA, sits over underground streams. People covered the streams with earth to make room for new buildings. Hundreds of years ago, people travelled through the city by canoe.

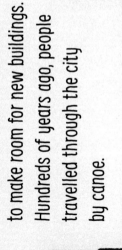

Hot and cold

Many underground pipes carry water. But this maze of pipes carries natural gas. Natural gas heats buildings in winter. During summer it cools them.

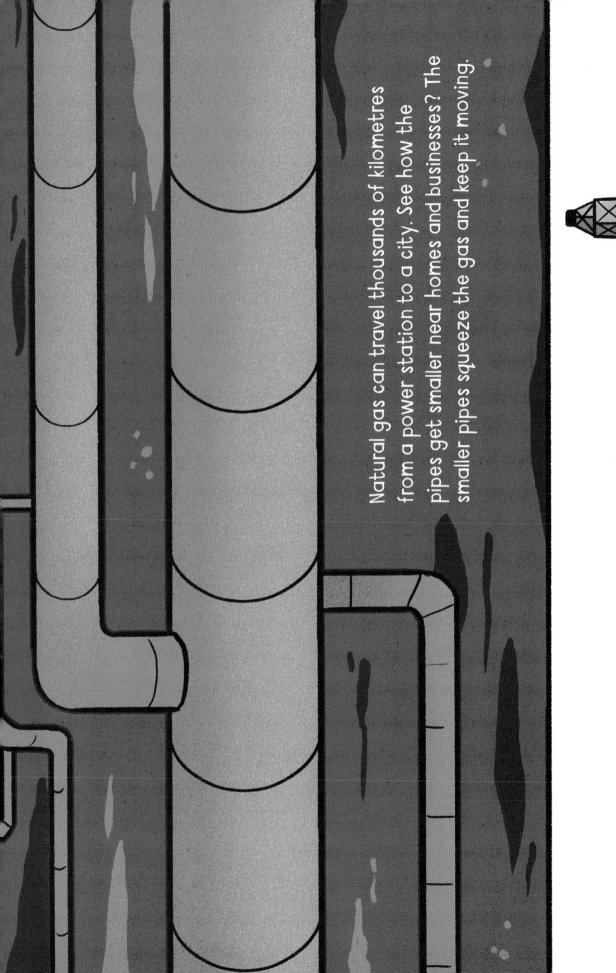

Natural gas can travel thousands of kilometres from a power station to a city. See how the pipes get smaller near homes and businesses? The smaller pipes squeeze the gas and keep it moving.

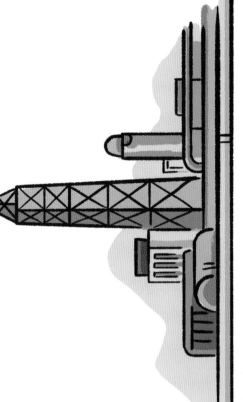

DID YOU KNOW?

Natural gas is a fossil fuel. People mine for natural gas by drilling deep into the Earth. Then power stations purify the gas and send it out to cities.

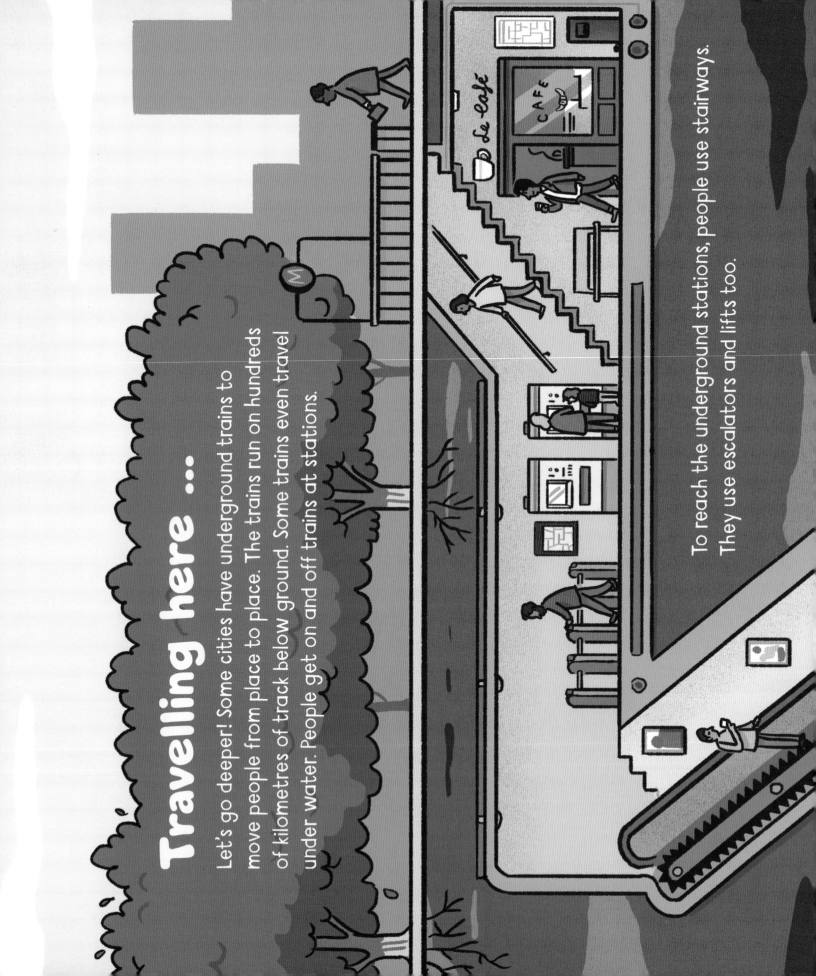

Travelling here ...

Let's go deeper! Some cities have underground trains to move people from place to place. The trains run on hundreds of kilometres of track below ground. Some trains even travel under water. People get on and off trains at stations.

To reach the underground stations, people use stairways. They use escalators and lifts too.

CAFE

le café

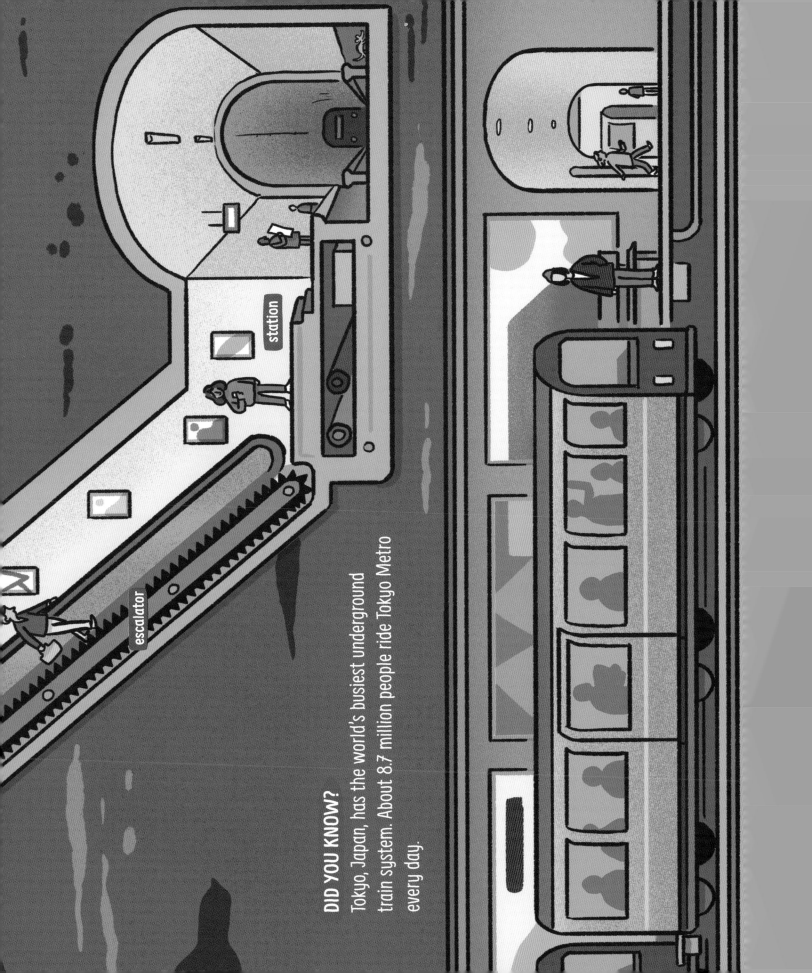

escalator

station

DID YOU KNOW?
Tokyo, Japan, has the world's busiest underground train system. About 8.7 million people ride Tokyo Metro every day.

And travelling there ...

Not all underground tunnels have railway tracks. Some tunnels hold roads. Putting roads underground leaves more space above ground for people to live.

Beneath Boston, Massachusetts, USA, cars zoom on motorways 8 to 10 lanes wide. To dig tunnels that deep and wide, workers moved a lot of earth. They filled more than 541,000 lorries!

Dino-rific!

Fossils are the remains of plants or animals from long ago. The remains sank deep into the earth. Over thousands of years they hardened into rock. Today when workers dig below cities, they often find fossils.

Sometimes the fossils are dinosaur bones. Builders in China once found **43** fossilized dinosaur eggs at their worksite.

How many eggs can you find here?

Laid to rest

crypt

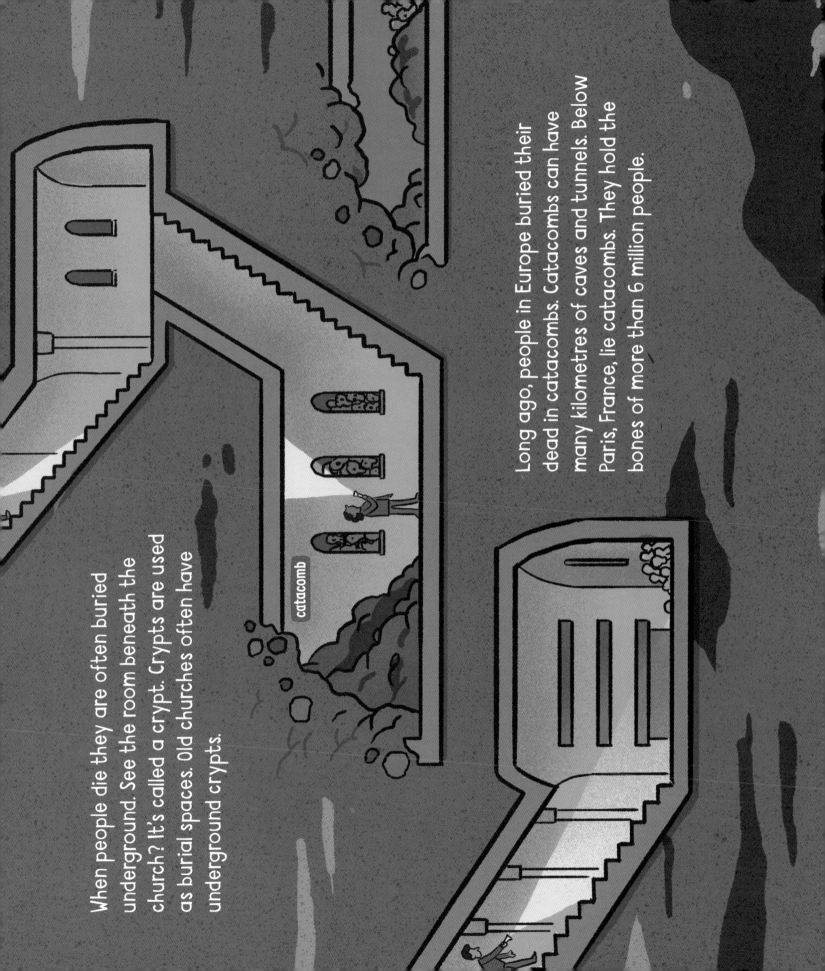

When people die they are often buried underground. See the room beneath the church? It's called a crypt. Crypts are used as burial spaces. Old churches often have underground crypts.

catacomb

Long ago, people in Europe buried their dead in catacombs. Catacombs can have many kilometres of caves and tunnels. Below Paris, France, lie catacombs. They hold the bones of more than 6 million people.

Standing tall

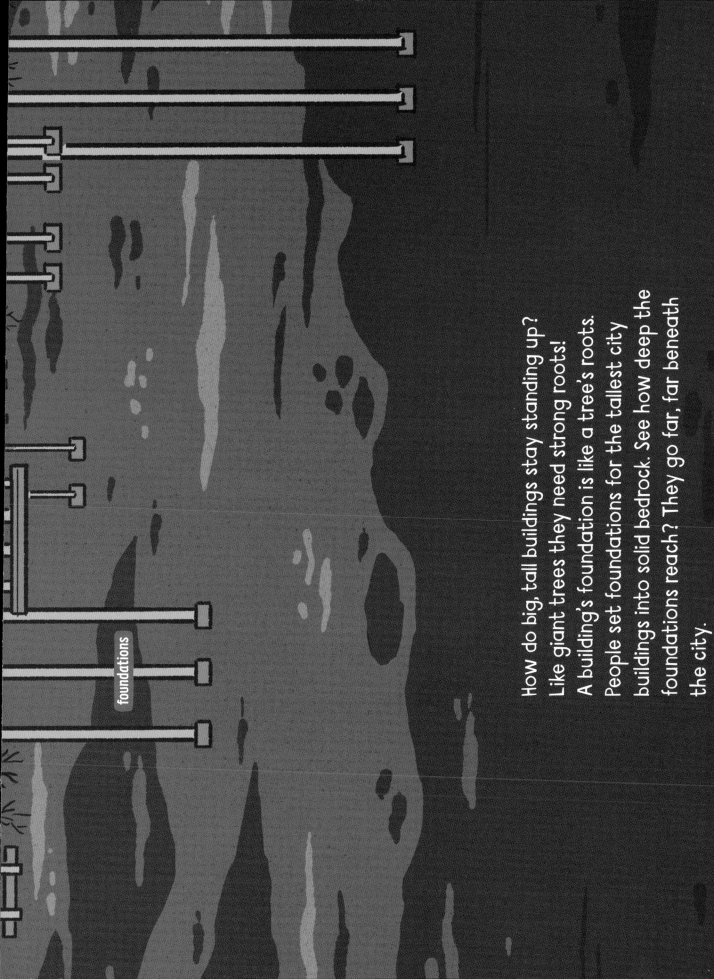

foundations

How do big, tall buildings stay standing up?
Like giant trees they need strong roots!
A building's foundation is like a tree's roots.
People set foundations for the tallest city
buildings into solid bedrock. See how deep the
foundations reach? They go far, far beneath
the city.

Goodbye, water

Clean water is necessary in our lives. So is getting rid of dirty water. Pipes carry waste from buildings to waste water treatment plants. Plant workers clean the water. Then they send it back to lakes and rivers.

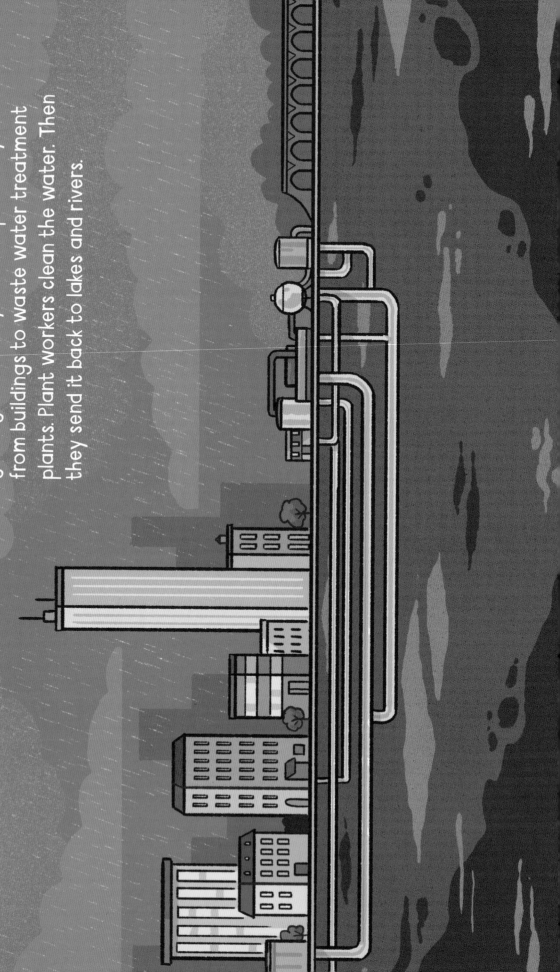

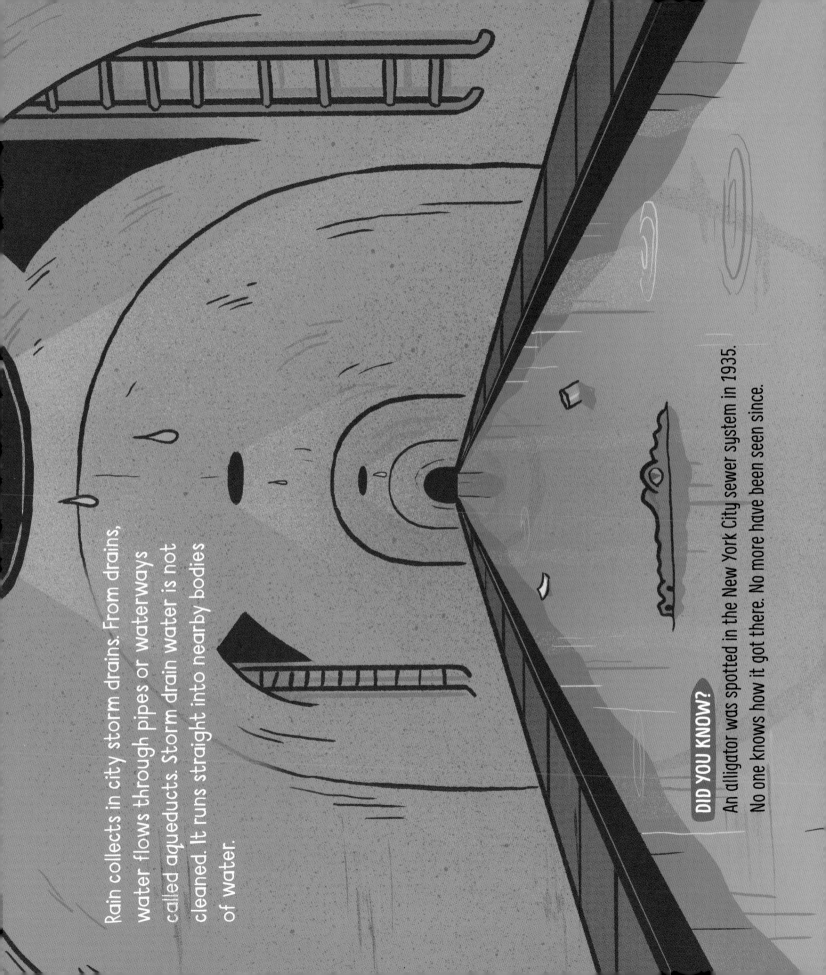

Rain collects in city storm drains. From drains, water flows through pipes or waterways called aqueducts. Storm drain water is not cleaned. It runs straight into nearby bodies of water.

Water supply

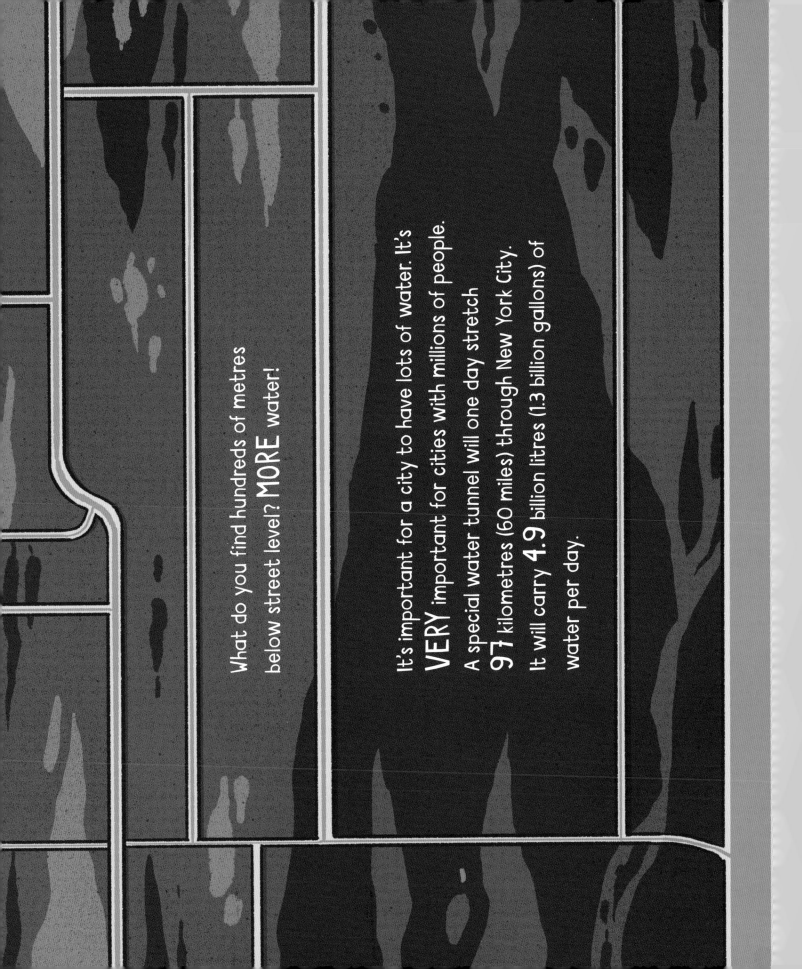

What do you find hundreds of metres below street level? **MORE** water!

It's important for a city to have lots of water. It's **VERY** important for cities with millions of people.

A special water tunnel will one day stretch **97** kilometres (60 miles) through New York City.

It will carry **4.9** billion litres (1.3 billion gallons) of water per day.

From long ago

You can find all sorts of things buried under a city. Bones, shells and fossils?

Of course!

You can find cannonballs, anchors and whole ships. Metal pipes, pottery and glass bottles might be there too. You might even find an entire ancient city! Scientists study the things they dig up. They use them to find out how people lived in the past. It's like exploring an underground museum.

How about full skeletons? Yes!

Coins and dishes? Sure!

Back on the street, cars honk, lights flash and people rush home for dinner. A city is a busy place above ground.

GLOSSARY

ancient from a long time ago

aqueduct large channel built to carry water

bedrock layer of solid rock beneath the layers of soil and loose gravel broken up by weathering

catacomb underground network of burial tunnels and chambers

civil engineer person who works on the design, construction or maintenance of any structure

conduit protective tube that contains wires and cables

crypt burial chamber

escalator moving staircase

fossil remains or traces of an animal or a plant, preserved as rock

fossil fuel natural fuel formed from the remains of plants and animals; coal, oil and natural gas are fossil fuels

purify make something clean

reservoir holding area for large amounts of water

sewer underground system of drains and pipes that carries dirty water

solar having to do with the sun

turbine engine powered by steam, water, wind or gas passing across the blades of a fan-like device and making it spin

FIND OUT MORE
BOOKS

In a City (Where I Live), Honor Hand (Wayland, 2010)

The London Underground Activity Book, Samantha Meredith (Scholastic, 2012)

Under the Ground (First Reading), Susanna Davidson (Usborne, 2010)

WEBSITES

primaryfacts.com/2522/london-underground-facts/

Visit this site to find out lots of facts about the London Underground.

www.yac-uk.org/news/what-is-archaeology

If you are interested in digging up the past, visit the website of the Young Archaeologists' Club to find out how you can get involved.

COMPREHENSION QUESTIONS

1. Why do you think power and information cables lie close to the surface and not deep underground?

2. Explain how drinking water gets to a building in a city.

3. What do civil engineers do? And why are they important?

Raintree is an imprint of Capstone Global Library Limited, a company incorporated in England and Wales having its registered office at 264 Banbury Road, Oxford, OX2 7DY – Registered company number: 6695582

www.raintree.co.uk
myorders@raintree.co.uk

Text © Capstone Global Library Limited 2016
The moral rights of the proprietor have been asserted.

ISBN 978 1 4747 1303 0
19 18 17 16 15
10 9 8 7 6 5 4 3 2 1

British Library Cataloguing in Publication Data
A full catalogue record for this book is available from the British Library.

Editorial Credits
Jill Kalz, editor; Russell Griesmer, designer; Nathan Gassman, creative director; Katy LaVigne, production specialist

Acknowledgements
We would like to thank Erin Santini Bell, PhD, PE, Civil Engineering, University of New Hampshire, USA, for her invaluable help in the preparation of this book.

Every effort has been made to contact copyright holders of material reproduced in this book. Any omissions will be rectified in subsequent printings if notice is given to the publisher.

All the Internet addresses (URLs) given in this book were valid at the time of going to press. However, due to the dynamic nature of the Internet, some addresses may have changed, or sites may have changed or ceased to exist since publication. While the author and publisher regret any inconvenience this may cause readers, no responsibility for any such changes can be accepted by either the author or the publisher.

Printed and bound in China.

LOOK FOR ALL THE BOOKS IN THE SERIES:

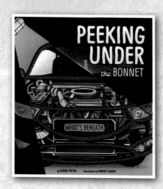